Trick Vessels

To Aida

Become a tree ———

Trick Vessels

Andre Bagoo

Andre Bagoo

London

2014

xxxx

Shearsman Books

First published in the United Kingdom in 2012 by
Shearsman Books
50 Westons Hill Drive
Emersons Green
Bristol
BS16 7DF

Shearsman Books Ltd Registered Office
30–31 St. James Place, Mangotsfield, Bristol BS16 9JB
(this address not for correspondence)

http://www.shearsman.com/

ISBN 978-1-84861-203-7

Contents

For my parents
Margaret Bagoo and Daniel Holder

The action of the device is as follows: three liquids of different colours are poured into a hole in the cover of the jar in succession; shortly after all the liquid has been poured in, the liquids discharge from an outlet pipe in the same succession. As is the case with Philo and Hero, the Banū Mūsā give few constructional details; dimensions are not given, nor are we told how the small tanks and other components inside the large jar were supported. Nevertheless, there is no doubt that these trick vessels were made, and experiments confirm that they would have worked.

—Donald Hill,
A History of Engineering in Classical and Medieval Times

Tissue and bones, it was a trick

—Grizzly Bear, 'Ready, Able'

The Night Grew Dark Around Us

Let the daughter of that hibiscus say:
"His love has no end."
Let the mother of the daughter say:
"His love has no end."
Let the author of the mother say:
"His love has no end."

Let the love, which is a flower, say:
"His love had no end."
Let the flower, which is the night, say:
"His love has no end."

The Unnamed Creature
Said to Come From Water

Give me two pairs of shoes, burn one on the beach
Dip the other at sea and then will you be free

Hear this: the ocean is not meant to be lit at night
Instead of going to water I go to light

I have swum in invisible ink for thousands of years
Liquid and air have parted, empty for centuries

Now I change your habit of playing in the rain
Now you come to learn the danger of lightning

I have figured out how to enter your dreams
I have deciphered the cipher for these trick vessels

The black voices sank and were drowned in the sea
The noises hush beneath the neon pool

Shackles chain you now, cup of tea in hand
Day dreaming by the water, feathers in the sand

At nights you sleepwalk here, where dank moths die
You walk in rain and wake up sweating, his lie

Your mother cannot name her great grandmother
Your father does not know where his village was

But I have such knowledge, I ensure these erasures
I follow the stop, I do not leak

Floating Vessels

Are stained white.
Black ink declared
All men to be equal but
Spines, rigged like chains,
Choked other limbs:
Feathered men
Replaced.

These vessels have knowledge
Where the sea ends.

Drains in Port of Spain
Flow where blue blood
Opens worlds.

Visa

for the world is defined by your island
your garden floods centuries away
over concrete jungle birds congregate
and the latitudes are crutches

where ideas come worlds leave me
soon words come and questions flee
when countries come I long for silence
in silence are memories of the sea

it was easy to imagine your island
a furniture wed to agile spies
    a stable is where they keep me
wrecked forever on memory

Landslide

What a stunning view.
Pity.

The land must now
redecorate itself,
                    pull the carpet out
shed
houses like yours.

The land must now
peel salt layers, put on
a corduroy mud jacket.

It does not need your help to dress.
Grow up.

What a pity about the house.
That stunning view of the sea.

How big a word, sea

Only three letters…

Cant

I

You forget it
        but it is true
  almost all of the earth
is covered with sand
pale grains tumble
under mountainous water
sustaining a thought
        across the centuries

whereas the stars are grains
whereas sleep takes me to them
whereas the eternal stretch is sleep
whereas your dog is a fur coat

      the dream breathes water
my hand gulps sand
  a bottle pounds the castle
knocking on the steel earth
  frothing
        making
a hollow noise

II

The man at the corner
     my eye is one
  the Three Kings

the streets of Belmont
  zigzag and then jump

walls that are waves
brick-tiled pink salmon

I tell left to right by the birthmark on my arm
The ghost beneath old newspaper photos

Consider the movement of this page
Caused by the shape of a poem

How the tips of white eyes
Have become black stops
        Pause when arrested
Stains

Contranyms are not discernable
Until it is too late. Versus

Moves towards its antithesis
        Two funerals for the King
                The missing sock is a key

                I no longer desire to ask questions
                But in silence more come
                But in silence more come
                But in silence more come
                        My mother
                        desired things

I want to sleep now
      until I reverse the outside
the burnt house he photographed
      trim from afar
turning to a ruin

An old man sits on the red love seat
      saved from the fire
For me to capture
With light

The Sea Emptied

i. Ms Jack's Daughter Leaves Us in Rage

In this crystal drain a fish grows
Until we abandon all things
Drain water of conversation
Clear softness of petals and weeds
As sure as that mossy drain:
She was enraged at broken terracotta men
Who picked plaster with scattered rain
A barren geography of drains
That the sea emptied
Now walls grow taller bodies

ii. Ms Jack's House Grows Wild Lungs

Held under by small hands
A floating plastic bag breathes salt
It swims away before it is named
A rose shawl freed of boats

Prefaces for Other Occasions

All Saints

  I will repent
I will
I will try to repeat this
In words developed below
In worlds too terrifying
I am terrorized
I am silenced
I am shadow
I see everything you don't love
I'll see all of the saints swimming
I'll see the sea
I'll drown this island
I will watch you go

Dedication of a Church

We, an awkward crown
Up-stretched arms for thorns
Spines as old as birthdays
Spire organs calcified
Where flutes breathe hymns
Stones spell with ink

We, an unworn crown
Quiet rivers worship gladly
A day that rumbles perpetually
Green mountains are fortified
Fibrous nerves whipped by light
Gems adorn nerve endings

We, an unadorned crown
A city of naked memories
In the diocese of endings
Bones bare castrati
Beautiful coral reefs
Submerged beneath sea

Baptism

There is a special way of being
afraid which no trick dispels

    The easy push of an open door
    The door that easily locks you in

Coral snake a string of pearls
The surfboard a wing
Arachnid flowers gold
Metal bones singing

Marriage

There is a special way of being
afraid which no trick dispels

No mirror satisfies
Amulets grow light

Zen white turns silver
Every body is pure

My body grows bronze
Locked in mahogany

Til you fly to the moon
Sipping vodka at the bar

Commemoration of the Dead

Dad is painting the family plot pink
Our Father who art in cemetery
Daily he wears punk trousers
Ripped shirt torn by green
Seduced by mossy angels
Made statuesque by salt

The dead don't want pink
They tell the rain to fall
They lure the sun out
The bristles of Greek wings
Fallen: father's brush

From the dead they will
From the dead light-bulbs turn off
From the dead on, then off
Til the pact is fulfilled

At nights I dream of mother
In different houses
At nights I dream of mother
Over the ocean
At nights I dream of mother
In your poem
At nights the water is cold
Your garden locked

To the Centre of the Earth

Q.

The sensation of the world is a trembling of water that gauges the smallness of the room. The space underneath is empty but for one thing: Luis the Goldfish who risks death by plastic seaweed. Corralled by dust and fish food, I linger to the surface. Whereas the mountain shaking is the centre of the earth signaling indifference, I love being shaken to the core.

A.

Is the sensation of the world a birdcage? The original state of the universe is a feather. Time has a barometer which records in pitch. All of the detritus of the past merges to form one marble, pitched in the dirt. It became sand which became ash and dust upon the asphalt yard of children lining up to kiss a second version of forever.

Q.

The aspect of the chair most likely to incriminate is its red. Everything leaves evidence. Skins. Furs. Fibers. The wheels will drop fragments, make a trail detectable only by the most impossible of eyes. And I will leave behind water and tea, and cookies and spelt grains…

A.

Small rooms are the best places for windows, they are so grateful. Like the children in the classroom. The classroom of small windows. The grateful children. The scene where the teacher held chalk. (At the back of the classroom is a cupboard, oozing secret passages.)

Q.

There is a pool in the room next door. There is another pool, nylon and blue in the emerald grass outside. The sound of water tumbling interrupts the calm surface outside: a dilemma.

A.

Upon it, at intervals, is the surface of the earth. A liquid mass so secret it has become solid. A shield that wraps an undigested magma. Blossoming black veins that irrupt in orange flowers and white lily ribbons.

Q.

Of course he is right. But if he is right, he is wrong. He says everyone is wrong. The evidence: Luis the Goldfish swimming outside in chlorine. The absence of salt.

A.

There is a room that moves inside of this one. It is inside the maker of the room. The maker of the room carries with her the last room she was in. The last room was across the Savannah, small and with a window. That room had white light. When the earthquake came, pictures fell and shattered and became real for one moment before extinction. She crouched under the doorway with no door. They say stand under doorways. The solid oak table was too small a space. *Imagine being trapped in a small space, beneath the surface of the earth. Imagine no light, and the old magazines they threw away which you stole and stacked here in towers, plunged under the detritus of small windows.* But when the hermit finds a new shell, there is always a moment when the creature is vulnerable. In between rooms, there is oblivion. A risk of freedom. A place with no geography and that bears no grudge against the centre of the earth. *Imagine the room now within her now within the room. And then a new skin; a new shell. This room is noisier.* The water of the fish pool next door is loud. It ripples on the pool outside. The sensation of the world is a trembling of water.

Q.

What is in the small bag in the hands of the children at the back of the class?

24

A.

The key to unlocking mystery is not making a fuss. The evidence is never irrefutable. Evidence is the foundation of everything. But it is a field wrought with dispute.

Q.

Deeper now, to the centre of everything. Luis the Goldfish has many colours. He, like the chair, was once red. Therefore, he was once orange and blue and purple. If you look carefully, everything is purple.

A.

Nothing. The fish-tank has many guests. The last one swam unto the bookcase and buried itself behind a glass sliding door. It sat next to the diamond sculpture that laughs, it opens the blue sky and turns these canyons of DVDs into hopes and memories. It would like to recall the hours before, though it will not remember even then. It is a crayon portrait on the bare wall, a clock, a coat of paint that matches a shawl, a loose lamp with white light. The TV, too, has a light to offer: black. The rustling of the room is a pulse, is a cavern. In the mysteries there are new gifts. In the mysteries there is an ocean in which the water will overwhelm. And will, infinitely, tremble. Like the trembling that marks the centre of a carrot when the metal blade meets.

Q.

The shell is painted gold. It is a magic shell. The children think it a key. So intent are they, it becomes a key. It unlocks the cupboard at the back of the classroom. Inside is the sensation of the known world. The sensation of the world is a trembling of water

Rooms

I

The most beautiful creature
Is the bottom feeder
Tiger claws for fins
Zebra stripes of Ikea cushion
That swim into a favorite pajama
Behind the shiny car window
Your purple and silk
They wear reflection well

II

There is not much to do
When your friends are all fish.
Invisible people at the offices
Work on being, on trying
On moving blinds and switches.
In this Central Bank fete jellyfish
Have anti-gravity suits, mingling
With twin towers that call out
Names, names, names.
                              Mercifully,
They hide a sea-sick melody.
With soft scaly bodies
With costumes made of blue
With cocktails and maraschino cherries
A moon full of copper.
The coral at the bar has a wish:
To reveal. Always, the same names.
Always, a wish.

III

Three tassa drummers in the small yard
Orchestrate a heist, with invisible actors
Playing the register in the grocery
Upstairs. In the dark, beans are on special,
With flashes of moving signs. The empty
Islands of cheap sweets, beaten raw,
Drum up red confections.
These liquid surfaces
Tell sweat where to go
Form pools of parlor sweets
Melted toffee and tamarind muscle.
My piece is heavy, thunder thighs
That are the weight of jealous lust
Burnt calories form invisible strands
Of golden hair, crowning.

IV

Soon spin class will be over
And I will repay all my sins
Piled up wet towels that smell
Like the most beautiful creature
The bottom feeder
Tiger claws for fins
Zebra stripes of Ikea cushion
They swim into a favorite pajama
Behind the shiny car window
Your purple and silk
It bears reflection well

Changeling

I give you my tongue that you may speak
That you may hear I give you my ear
I give you my skin for you to feel
Feet so you may walk

Speak, that I may have a tongue
Hear and I may have ears
Feel that I may grow skin
Write for these legs to be complete

The Oilbird

On the morning Christ died
we eat the eggs of birds
white china offers incense
as coffee wakes the dead.
In deep forest they walk
steps marking trails
concrete slabs crawl
escaping green longing.
Do you come
like the jar flies do?
Will your soul leave
a molt decoy too?
I heard you in the night
talking about dying
they said you were a jumbie
bird, I knew better.
I knew the gorge you came from
that it was not a cave
there was a small space for light
in the dark of dirt rock.
       Perched on wet stone
with stubby feet and
an eagle's royal coat
your wings grow eternal.
There is only one fruit
you shall ever eat.
There is only one time
you shall ever fly.
Your young are slit
to fuel the light
when all your life
is bright darkness.

These cave screams
are flight, entombed
on Easter Sunday.
They rise.

On Shadowing and Reading Dew

Dressing and disguising yourself can help you in a surveillance,
especially if the person you are following or staking out is you.
A female is nowhere near as obtrusive as a male. That's one reason
I have female agents. We put the female in the shotgun position.
Obviously she's waiting for her husband. Not a problem.
When going on surveillance always take a change of clothes—
sometimes several changes of clothes. If you anticipate your subject
may be going to the beach, bring along a swim suit, towel, shorts,
and shirt—anything you may need to fit in. A jacket is a tool
to change the colour of what you are wearing.
Prepare a cover story in case you're spotted. Have your identity ready.
Walk with a dog leash. If they ask for your dog tell them he ran away
and you are looking for him. Know your own name, where you live, etc.
Tip: Lack of dew on a vehicle during morning hours could indicate
it was moved sometime that night.
Verify address by looking at the mailbox for a name or peeking
at the mail if it's sticking out. Determine whether residence is a
single or multi-family home by counting # of electric meters.
How many adults were around you as a child who should not have
        been?
While tailing someone, you notice the person stopping in front of a
        house.
You (i.e. your cover) continue past, turn into an empty driveway
as if you belong there. Take detailed notes via pen & paper or voice
        recorder.
You will lose it all, like love. When running video, there will be lots of
stop starting of the camera—create definite borders between clips by
placing a hand over the camera at the end of each segment. I call this
putting a hand to hush a mouth. You need this to remember memories
you will forget.

Fuddling Cup

My friend is he
who loves me well
but who he is
I cannot tell

I cannot tell
Who he is

Who he is
I cannot tell

Gluttony Cup

You should know when to stop.

Pot Crown

Thorns are replaced with beer.

When the cup runneth over,
the crown must be gingerly placed
on the head of the object:

Only then can those in admiration
attempt to exercise their skill
in emptying the cup.

The endeavours of the undesirable ones
are easily foiled
by the object moving its head ever so little
like the turn of the forged key.

In this galactic cell-tower, the liquid must be still
it must chance a heartbeat
that can drain the evaporating contents
by drawing the liquor up.
There is a hidden tube.

Dutch Courage

The Stag needs a mate
To keep it company.
It's sweating,
It might be crying,
Either way it's wet
And frothy and pithy and bitter
But not too much
Like its price.
The Stag needs a mate
Who will not just drink it
Who might slowly peel off
The black, red and gold
Label, and use the label
As art, and make a sign
That says, 'this is not just a Stag'.
This Stag does not want to be
A Carib, a Heineken or Stella.
But it is the moment when it
Is not itself that it is most itself;
When it is opening a bottle
And drinking a beer and
Saying stupid things
And getting really drunk
And getting really free
And getting lost
And getting green
Before taking the beer and
Making a punch
Drunk resolution
To resolutely resolve.
The peeled label spills—
Liquid spells on your lap,
'This is not just yours.'

Tusks

it prints dust
cracks pavements
doors opened by it
houses entered by it
silent living rooms

a hunter is murdered
a mate found
ivory stolen

blood on the doors

                shadows

Seven Acts of Mercy

Caravaggio's cherubs fucking on the roof
A nipperkin pours deception
The poem unmasks itself
You can fill this if you want
The puzzle jug is half-empty
There is no liquid here
What were the seven acts exactly?

A Window at KFC, Frederick Street, Near to a Gaol

The child asks the woman—who
might be a sister mother aunt   cousin
neighbour social worker or stranger—where
are the people going?
       Everyday the same people pass.
Everyday the child is at the window.
Each day the woman.
Where are they going?
The woman asks the man—
who might be employed at KFC or who might be
Her husband brother cousin   son
Boyfriend or random stranger—a question.
Where do they come *from*?
       I think to myself:
It must be the same place;
All of them come everyday.
Someone makes an observation:
It must be the same thing they are looking
For.
    They must not find it ever.
What are they looking for?
What do they find?
If they had found it
they would not move.

Capital

The citizens are all vagrants
Sleep on cardboard floors
Shelter under paper roofs
Graffiti of muck for signage
Parliament's public bathroom

I used to live next to the Globe
In a narrow space between billboards
It gnawed my ankle
Now steel and glass blow glitter
Twenty-five stories new
Shimmering Carnival standards
On the feted Waterfront

I was dragged by anchor chain
Back to a landlocked fountain
A feather awaits me

Golden Grove

every door
every grey cell
every iron bar and gate
every column of windows
every seat in this airless chapel

of throbbing bodies
is mute

every soldier
every gun
every blade of brown grass
every cracked glass

pane
through which a child's report card
must be red
is silent

every mahogany louvre
every lookout tower
every tile on
every floor

is wanting—
not a single ripe fruit
not a trace of gold leaf
not a tree

in Golden Grove
there are colonies within this colony
blocks C to D to E

where one by one the progeny
of my great grandfather
come
to die excellently

here
the strongest of bodies are dazed
beneath showers of diamond sprinkles
a thousand cold handcuffs
fall on black limbs
men are clothed in blue
to mark them as 'lifers':
really condemned

unused condoms mark the territory
behind the kitchen
where for Fathers' Day all the dads
would get to see their children
and all the children and wives and lovers
would be brought into Golden Grove

Carnival

You are not my mother so you hold
my hand tighter than you should.

The wind blows my Indian feather,
And throws red dust into my face.

This is supposed to be fun, but when
We reach the Savannah stage I am terrified.

Your son, my half brother, is cold
He does not chip to the dollar wine.

This Kiddies Carnival experiment
Has gone awry. I've lost my axe.

You say you have to leave me here
It is five o'clock and Panorama is tonight.

You are going and my father is going
But my mother is staying home and

I am staying home to wash all this
Glitter and Vaseline off my small body.

Somewhere near that Savannah stage
The crowds crush my black cardboard axe.

Aid

To crawl is to dig is to breathe
dirt. The oxygen is rock.

Looting becomes living
as waterfronts overflow:
twenty-five stories clap.

Empty palaces will eat you
freed rubble, filled.
If the walls did not kill you
the now missing will.

How to Put a Cat into a Hypnotic Trance

I think my cat has been hypnotized.
I looked it up on the internet.
People believe it is difficult to hypnotize cats,
But hypnotizing a cat is easier than hypnotizing people.
It is also easier than hypnotizing chickens.
I have tried.

The first step to hypnotize a cat
is to build rapport with it and become its friend.
Do so by feeding, playing, stroking or talking to it
smoothly with a calm voice.
Build friendly communication and gain trust.
If the cat doesn't accept you,
it will be difficult.

After you build a rapport with the cat,
gently lay it down on its favorite side.
Stroke it for some minutes,
keep it in a lying position with your other hand.
But if the cat wants to get up, don't force it:
continue building trust
through friendly communication.
If you build enough trust,
then the cat will easily comply
when you lay it down.

Continue to stroke the cat and calm it this way.
Do this for some minutes.
After it is quite still, stop stroking and remove
your other hand, too.
Now your cat is in a hypnotic trance.
This is an excellent therapy.

And This Note Was Not an Answer

For this was the first time I questioned anything
And the more I questioned the smaller
The questions grew.
      The less questions are asked
the more they grow.
Each question begets violence.
It begs on behalf of its recipient.
Like the silence of the blank note
Returned in answer to
The questions that knew.

The Marble Altar

Even in this church
They crawl the walls
As though at his room:
A silent trail of thousands
That bite like empty vessels
Used to extract blood.

In this church,
The walls bleed
The crumbling walls, painted
Apple white, give birth to
Our Lady in tears.

Five years old and crying
In the corner of a wall
Dripping apple skin
Dented corner of forehead.

Five years old and crying
The cheap painting of a boat at sea
Breaks his jaw, poetically.

And here are these red ants, here
Among these pine pews, clawed,
And those Stations of the Cross
(Genuflections and more and more!)
As mother walks to the altar.

My Father's Car

My father's car is white, it looks split

In two; put together with spit,

Glue, and grey potty goo. I broke

the radio antenna, and said, "I

think I broke your radio antenna," (though

I was convinced this was untrue, I

think I broke it for spite, to spite and despite

you). I think I broke you, am not sure who

broke this in two. We sit back,

black asphalt rolling beneath us, a lack

of talk, a big sexy backseat, a dangling rosary:

We are going to church, but the gas tank is empty.

There is a taste of wafer on my tongue;

A stickiness all over my sweaty body.

I try to remember the name

Of the gospel song on the radio as we

Turn into a gas station. The attendant doesn't see

me. He crows to you.

You ask me to pay

—you're broke, you say.

Prima Facie

I: *Eighth Magistrate's Court*

They do murder here
Behind three sets of
Double doors, in a dock
Where a cousin of Derek
Walcott sits mumbling
Prayers over hot zaki beads
In perfect rhyme and metre
Next to prisoners wearing gowns
Accessorised by silver bracelets
While the guards wear latex
Gloves like powdery condoms
And fully dressed lawyers
Soliloquize casually—all
Black.

The accused did walk out dead
He walked back in dead,
Dead man and his victims:
Lawyers, magistrates, lovers—dead,
Where death is done with none.

II: *(Memories of Asia LaLuna)*
or I wished my father was a rich lawyer

The message from the drag queen was:

*"It just came to our attention that there is a rumour going
around that my dear Auntie Suzie and me got into a heated
squabble the night of the Diva Duels challenge. I want to*

state emphatically that nothing of the sort occurred and that I hold Aunty Wednesday in very high esteem. I was thoroughly surprised to find mention of my person on a blog, where I was slandered with unfounded and unconfirmed rumours (the person's inability to spell my name also irked me). Nevertheless, I am asking that this self proclaimed Queen Mother sit down with Asia LaLuna for an in-depth one on one to get the facts straight!"

I remembered it in court, as the barrister, in cobo pleats, was talking about bias.
I wish my dad was a rich lawyer, I thought, so I could do things.
Lord Hope, the cobo said, had once said:

"The fair-minded and informed observer is a relative newcomer among the select group of personalities who inhabit our legal village. Like the reasonable man whose attributes have been explored so often in the context of the law of negligence, the fair-minded observer is a creature of fiction. Gender-neutral (because in this case the complainer and the person complained about are both women, I shall avoid using the word "he"), she has attributes which many of us might struggle to attain to."
"The observer who is fair-minded is the sort of person who always reserves judgment on every point until she has seen and fully understood both sides of the argument. She is not unduly sensitive or suspicious. But she is not complacent either. She knows that fairness requires that a judge must be, and must be seen to be, unbiased. She knows that judges, like anybody else, have their weaknesses."

A real possibility is far less than a probability.
The days stretched out before me smell like meat.
Opening a diary does terrible things to you.

"It's in the bundle at tab 96, meh lord."
"Would you like to refresh your memory?"

The room next door is a red lava heart.
I smell guava, hoping that robes matter.
Hundreds of downy robes pleat with pride.
We are all called at some time.

III: *Third Magistrates' Court*

Is the place I sit to get some peace.
The mad man once pelted the Magistrate here
With a bag of his own shit.
Found life too shitty, apparently.
I like to remember him.
It smells of vinegar.
Or is it wine?

The House Was Really Falling from the Sky

To show the house falling from the sky,
a miniature house was dropped onto a sky
painting on the stage floor, then
the film was reversed to
show the house was really falling from the sky
not towards the glass air.

Sundays

It is always on Sundays that bomb blasts kill
sleep
    that you eat after praying
for those absent at the table
they sit here and eat your
  water drink
your rice and peas

      bombasts long last
in memory
where guilt lingers longer
in conspiracy
with feet beneath
Sunday tables

Dribble Cup

Dear R—, I am sure that I am going to disappoint you with what I am about to write. I am so appreciative of the offer you made me. The idea of three weeks spent at your house at Toco was a wonderful one. But I cannot leave the building. As you know, I have a great many enemies. Besides, the last time I was in Toco, I had a dream about talking to an owl. The owl asked me who I was. I didn't think that was funny.

Anyhow, the disappointing news--well not really disappointing, it depends on how you look at the object--is that I've decided not to pursue my studies in the law. Instead, I am going to study magic. Hope you didn't spill the tea you must have been sipping while you read this. You have to admit that in a sense you must have expected it. Remember how there was the man at the races who always used to come to me and tell me, "you've got the magic?" That was a sign all along. And how do you think we managed to win all those hams that year at the college Mayfair?

Anticipating your support, I've already enrolled in a fine program. I think it's GATE-approved, but am not certain. The university has accreditation and their diploma is recognized all over the world. They offer a product tailored to my needs. Could you get the following items for me?

COMPULSORY COURSE MATERIALS:

1. One Bar Bug in an Ice Cube
2. One Squirting Coin
3. One Laughing Tissue
4. A box of Cachoo Sneezing Powder

5. *A pack of Exploding Cigarette Boxes*
6. *Three Snake Nut Cans*
7. *Itching Powder*
8. *A Stink Bomb*
9. *A Joy Buzzer (check Amazon.com)*
10. *Something full of holes.*

Afterwards

2.

Spring water that tastes toxic.
Lunching on breakfast.
Thinking of not walking alone.
Running on a street that is longer.
Fearing the stop will pass you.
Confusing the last house with the next.
Eyeing the pissy walls.
Thinking of five minutes for five hours.
Saying it is nine o'clock to three.
Wanting to rest, but restless.
Throwing up petals and nails.
Falling for a trick, a wish.
Wishing sunset was sunrise.
Wishing the dead bat was not.

1.

Underwear on a clothes line, drying.
A ball the colour of the grey street, rolling.

Children running for a ball that passes where they hang.
You thought someone was next to you but he's not.

It is late and you were hoping what you said made sense.
Hoping to make recompense for what you said far too late.

Before it's too late you want to catch the ball that passes.
You don't want to pass your stop and then come undone.

You want to undo talk and trousers and knickers.
We hang limp and faded the day after on the line.

You want to lick the colour back in with your hands.
You want your hands to do the talking tonight.

3.

Like a haircut
Snowballs rolling down a bib
Like ashen lava
Like a memory,
          sinking
Like a feather, a drum
Like droplets of pleasure
The taste of skin,
A melody, a freedom
A light-headedness
A forgotten forgetfulness
Bright stars, blue moons
Eyes like eclipses
Like a grandmother
Like a kiss

Watermelon

(with apologies to Carol Ann Duffy)

Forget onions
my love is like a watermelon
wet, unwieldy, full of seed
yet refreshing and sweet
even if green.

My love is like a watermelon:
heavy, thick-skinned, rotund,
unseen among the vines
that mark the sharp ground.

A watermelon is like an onion:
layers give way to beneath
like a poem where words give way
to what is beneath.
What is beneath is often love.

A watermelon is not like an onion:
one is smelly, one creates fear.
But a watermelon is like my love
and the onion that brings a tear.

Prefaces for Seasons

Advent

I memorise every knot
Of these memorial pews
A baptism of Rough Tops
A silence shall be kept
Through corridors made of ants
There is a church inside a church
Where a mountain clump breaks off
And then

Incarnation

        becomes a tree
The tree that breaks free
To become a memory

You tell me to write a poem about the hill
      A jet dog appears
At first bitumen
Then furry gravel
Bitters grow brown
Orangutan green
Razor blades drape
This burnt Calvary

Epiphany

You tell me to write a poem about the dream
The priest was coming for me over the water
The lone thread of a spider's web
That trips and drapes time with words

The world was made flesh
And dwelt among us
Until the sun realised and told

Lent

The valuable becomes valueless

    In auctions the world is reversed

The desired is at first rejected

    The rejected is later consumed

The losers give nothing

    The winners pay everything

    or this:

You bid your faithful people cleanse their hearts, and
prepare with joy for the Paschal feast; that, fervent in prayer
and in works of mercy, and renewed by your Word and
Sacraments, they may come to the fullness of grace which
you have prepared for those who love you.

Holy Week

On Christmas Eve you can hear the dreams
Painting thinners, wrapping baking hams

The fish, ovened too soon, flakes
Lakes of Christmas lights

During these Blackberry weeks
At nights, when I awake, you glow red

Sorrel boiled fluorescent
Burning like touching hands

Thousands of touching hands
Covers for secret agents

In double worlds that sink beneath soil
Drilled in reverse are my steps

Straws crushed on the manger wall
Seeds buried in the tropics grow

Fruit that should not blossom here:
Apples, peaches, grapes for Holy Week

Easter

In between dreams
I make sense
In waking life
Chaos is hard to prove

Ascension

Millions die
We talk only of the living

To smile at funerals
To open half doors
Inner caskets

Satin cakes with secret
Cities of gold
Plunged low by a vacuum
      A line reversed
A gangly pipe of chill words

                  spilling

Spilt   split
          and spoilt
Risen to the soil
Beneath a floating island
Of hummingbird tar

Pentecost

At La Brea, a pond glides on the tar
Netting golden dragonfly wings
I hold a cup of oil for forty-nine days
Drop a little on water: baptism of crude fire
Spread swiftness on the surface
Like Jesus and his loaves
But oil did not soothe water
Make this diamond smooth
Leeward side is where waves are greatest
Leeward depends on windward to be true
The wind drove oil back on the shore
Ponds are always rejecting waste

On the fiftieth day my cup fell
And a teaspoon produced instant calm
At first a few yards square
Then a quarter of the pond
As smooth as a looking glass
In calm bed sheets

Bolt

For Antonia

"Can you hear the birds?"
"They are fighting on the roof."
"Come and take a picture for me."
"They are eating the house."
"Come and see them quick and take two pictures, please."
"They are eating the small rain-flies that shed wings."
"They are singing in the rain."
"The sky is very grey today, and very bright."
"Look at the yellow beaks. And the green."
"They look like puppets."
"They look like macaws."
"There are no parrots in this country."
"Of course there are parrots. And hummingbirds."
"I would take a picture of a hummingbird."
"Hummingbirds are too quick."
"The Gods buried people in tar because of hummingbirds."
"You can trap a hummingbird in a flower with glue."
"I know."
"It will have a heart attack."
"What is that?"
"It is downstairs."
"It is the sound of the ice shifting."
"A voice is shifting in the freezer."
"I unplugged the freezer."
"I mopped up the cold water."
"It is the sound of ice falling in the fridge."
"It is an iceberg breaking."
"It is thunder rolling."
"I cannot play in the rain today."
                    [ginger tea]
"If you play the lightning can strike you."

"But the birds are in the rain."
"Take a photo of them, quick."
"They are not hummingbirds."
"Can you see the wings?"

Trick Vessels

I. The Secret Cliff

swim too far you fall
off the secret cliff
that starts another world
where rivers flowed once

sip by accident you swallow
gulps of infested liquid
an itching throat is unbearable
sand flies gorging blood

stop here and never resume
buried memories shifty
the sea drinks more and more
not satisfied with laughter

II. Ti-Marie

I've been gulping sea-spray,
Walking along this country road,
Where a jumbie bird promises little deaths, like fireflies,
Where the asphalt, peeled,
Exposes tiny canyons of silver and quartz,
    And a pothole that leads
To the other side of the world.

I've been walking on this country road,
With walls of razor grass hiding gorges
Where heavy fruit fall like people in heat,
Where I stroke ti-marie, *morivivi,*
And it folds its arms, shy love.

They put dead bodies in that field, you say.
You—like the others—are always smiling.
Little teeth like steel girders
Link an imaginary highway, bridging Toco
       And Tobago.
The road forks where the
Bird of Paradise burns.

You, or one of you, take me,
      Or one of me,
To the lighthouse at the end of this road
Where slate rocks break
Like communion wafers between fingers;
Waves foam on a giant scrubbing stone
And in the ocean ship by ship falls
Off the edge of the secret cliff—

III. An Author's Note on Trick Vessels Which

Are not the same as impossible objects
The solutions are found in different places

And what is impossible changes
When it meets the ocean's surface

      For sure the trick vessel turns chances
All choices are not predetermined

But a trick vessel is never filled
Without secrets

65

IV. On Encountering Crapauds at Night

I've grown to love the backs of crapauds
That hide in dark spaces between steps
And bow as though at temple

In a giant conundrum
They sing and skip like sleepwalkers
Trapped in trick vessels

I could stare forever at crapaud back
Moth eyes but no wings
Smoking pipe

In the morning he kneels
His frail fingers are stuck
Like the toads praying outside

In the shower there are moths
That die under water
At nights, crapauds get hungry

V. The Man From Rio Claro

I am the man from Rio Claro, so the barman says.
The bar is not on fire, according to my friends.
The cloud under the roof is steam not smoke.
The smoking beer is ice-cold.
Five concrete steps lead nowhere,
        A place where I am unknown.
I am just passing.

I am the man from Rio Claro, so the barman says.
The smoke of my cigarette gnaws my clothes.
   I am easily inflamed.
At nights, the cigales spurt gasoline.
   A touch, and I am afraid.
The building is made of wood.
There's no water in Rio Claro.

VI. Journey By Night

The fig tree could be a murderer
A bandit come to ambush

The last time you walked this far
You were almost killed

You were almost killed in a car
You have survived so far

A screen, like the ones on doors,
Falls over the toady road

Netting fireflies that could be stars
Or Venus, a star-sign multiplied

A soft whisper can bite
A touch go far

Fireflies live just weeks
With impostors they die

VII. Horoscope

"...We tend to exaggerate
our feelings today.
The demonstrative Leo Moon reveals
our insecurities
stressfully aspecting four planets.

The challenge: to maintain a healthy
perspective about what we want
versus what we need
as sensual Venus creates
a crunchy quincunx
to indulgent Jupiter.

Meanwhile, a smoothly flowing trine
between Venus and passionate Pluto
allows us to incorporate
darker emotions
into a deep friendship or
an intimate relationship..."

VIII. Before Sequels

Book One of notepads with red ants crawling.
Book One of moths having sex.
Book One of the cook who says she used dynamite
        to shatter the earth and look for oil.
Book One of the knock that came from two doors.
Book One of a jep on the Lifebuoy soap in the washbasin.
Book One of seven steps with seven crapauds.

Book One's protagonist stands at the corner in bushes
        kissing a lover or eating a mango or talking to a jumbie.
Book One of sixteen hidden steps, in an uneven yard,
        that lead to more steps with more crapauds.
Book One where at the side of the road a pup drinks.
Book One is an atlas.
Book One is a puzzle forgotten if you do not write this down.
Book One has at last quelled allergic erections.
Book One of when the poet slips, calls the wrong country home.
Book One where Amerindian ancestors have come back as dogs.
Book One that must already be writ.

This Is a Gift for Someone
Who Will Not Have It

It is the jet puppy I have not seen before now
Whose name I do not know
Whose owner I do not know
Whose lover I do not know
Which walked the streets when
You dropped me home
Which you have just praised
Appraised described as a sausage
And asked if you could steal

This gift is for one who will not have it
From someone who will not give it
For someone who was not given to take it
Because to receive it is to give it
The promised endless barter

Thanks

Gratitude and love to Courtenay B. Williams. Warm thanks to Tony Frazer, Nicholas Laughlin, Helen Drayton, Therese Mills and the facilitators of the 2010 Cropper Foundation Writers Workshop, including Professor Funso Aiyejina and Dr Merle Hodge and all of the participants of that year's workshop. Especial thanks to: Lesann, Jaime, Danelle, Mike, Luke, Gingy, Fédon, Arden, Leila.

This book is for my parents, Margaret Bagoo and Daniel Holder.

Acknowledgements

Grateful acknowledgement is made to the editors of the following publications in which versions of some of the poems in this collection first appeared:

Boston Review ('Carnival');
Caribbean Review of Books ('Changeling', 'The Night Grew Dark Around Us');
St Petersburg Review ('The Unnamed Creature Said to Come From Water');
The Caribbean Writer ('Aid', 'Golden Grove');
tongues of the ocean ('My Father's Car', 'Watermelon').